360
595.7

FEB 04 2016

Winchester Public Library
Winchester, MA 01890
781-721-7171
www.winpublib.org

D1567590

ANIMAL CANNIBALS

Praying Mantises

Sam Hesper

PowerKiDS press.

New York

Published in 2015 by The Rosen Publishing Group, Inc.
29 East 21st Street, New York, NY 10010

Copyright © 2015 by The Rosen Publishing Group, Inc.

All rights reserved. No part of this book may be reproduced in any form without permission in writing from the publisher, except by a reviewer.

First Edition

Editor: Caitie McAneney
Book Design: Michael J. Flynn

Photo Credits: Cover Czesznak Zsolt/Shutterstock.com; p. 5 Lightspring/Shutterstock.com; p. 6 wiangya/Shutterstock.com; pp. 7, 14 Cathy Keifer/Shutterstock.com; p. 9 John Cancalosi/Photolibrary/Getty Images; p. 11 Medford Taylor/National Geographic/Getty Images; p. 13 Lakeview Images/Shutterstock.com; pp. 15, 17 Kristina Postnikova/Shutterstock.com; p. 19 kevin connors/Shutterstock.com; p. 20 Ryan M. Bolton/Shutterstock.com; p. 21 Evgeniy Ayupov/Shutterstock.com; p. 22 Peter Schwarz/Shutterstock.com.

Library of Congress Cataloging-in-Publication Data

Hesper, Sam, author.
 Praying mantises / Sam Hesper.
     pages cm. — (Animal cannibals)
 Includes index.
 ISBN 978-1-4777-5773-4 (pbk.)
 ISBN 978-1-4777-5775-8 (6 pack)
 ISBN 978-1-4777-5771-0 (library binding)
 1. Praying mantis—Juvenile literature. I. Title.
 QL505.9.M35H47 2015
 595.7'27—dc23
                                      2014027651

Manufactured in the United States of America

CPSIA Compliance Information: Batch #CW15PK: For Further Information contact Rosen Publishing, New York, New York at 1-800-237-9932

Contents

Praying Mantises

Praying mantises get their name because of the way they hold their front legs. They look like people praying. Praying mantises are often called mantises or mantids, and they are insects.

Insects are living things that have six legs and three body parts. The antennae, or feelers, on their head help them sense their surroundings. Most insects have wings, and most praying mantises have wings, too.

Praying mantises are predators, which means they hunt other animals for food. These creepy critters mainly eat insects. Praying mantises are also cannibals. That means they eat their own kind. Yuck!

Unlike other insects, praying mantises can turn their head all the way behind them. This helps them see in all directions.

Thousands of Species

There are around 2,300 species, or kinds, of praying mantis. Most praying mantises are green or brown, but mantises of other colors live around the world. One example is the orchid mantis, which looks like a purple or pink flower.

orchid mantis

Orchid mantises don't necessarily live on flowers. They look like flowers, though. That's enough to fool **prey**, such as butterflies, into coming near them.

devil's flower mantis

FOOD FOR THOUGHT

Praying mantises can be blue, purple, or even more than one color. Some mantis species are among the most colorful of all insects!

Have you ever seen a praying mantis? They're usually about a half inch to six inches (1.3 to 15.2 cm) long. Mantises have skinny bodies and heads shaped like triangles. Some mantis species have wings that look like leaves, and others look like bark. Scientists discover new species of praying mantis all the time!

Mantises at Home

Praying mantises live in **temperate** and **tropical** areas. They live on every continent except Antarctica because it's too cold there. Praying mantises like warm surroundings, and many live in rain forests around the world. Rain forests are warm and wet, and plenty of other insects live there, too.

Praying mantises love having other insects around because they make great meals. A rain forest is the perfect place for praying mantises to hunt, especially for the ones that **disguise** themselves as leaves, such as the hooded mantis. Found in Mexico and South America, these mantises hide among leaves until an insect falls for their disguise.

This hooded mantis blends in with the leaves. Would you be able to spot it?

A Mantis Body

Insects are invertebrates. This means they don't have a backbone like humans do. Instead, all insects—including praying mantises—have a hard outer covering. This outer covering, called an exoskeleton, holds and **protects** the soft inside parts of an insect, such as the heart.

Praying mantises usually have two sets of wings. One set is for flying, and it's very **delicate**. The other set protects the flight wings when the mantis isn't flying. Mantises have two big eyes with three smaller eyes between them. They have great vision because of how big their eyes are and how far they can turn their heads.

FOOD FOR THOUGHT

Female mantises are usually bigger than males. Many female mantises don't fly because they're too heavy. Besides, the males are always willing to come to them!

The wings of male praying mantises are usually bigger than the wings of female praying mantises. Males often fly in search of females.

Defenses

Praying mantises are built to hunt, but they're also prey for other animals. Do you think monkeys are cute? You might think so, but praying mantises don't! Some monkeys like to eat praying mantises. Birds, snakes, lizards, spiders, and bats hunt praying mantises, too.

Luckily, praying mantises have some special **defenses**. Their great vision helps them watch for and escape from predators. Another praying mantis defense is camouflage. This means they blend into their surroundings, making them hard to see. The orchid mantis looks like a flower to trick its predators. Camouflage also comes in handy when the orchid mantis is hunting.

Some praying mantises like to hunt at night because there are fewer predators awake to eat them.

FOOD FOR THOUGHT

Praying mantises have one ear in their **abdomen**. They can hear the call of a bat and can tell if the bat is chasing them. This sometimes keeps the mantises safe!

13

Hungry Hunters

A mantis's great vision keeps it safe, but also helps it hunt. Praying mantises don't have very good balance when they walk. But they're good at standing still and then striking quickly at their prey.

When a mantis watches its prey, it's called stalking. When it surprises the prey, it's called ambushing. They're both great hunting skills!

When hunting, a mantis lies very still and waits. It watches its surroundings until an insect appears. Then—snap! The mantis grabs its prey with its quick front legs.

Mantises have sharp points on their legs that make it hard for prey to escape. Some praying mantises bite their prey in the neck to **paralyze** them before chowing down.

What's on the Menu?

What's worse than eating insects for breakfast? How about eating live insects for breakfast? Praying mantises will snatch a cricket or bee from the air and eat it on the spot. Mantises have strong mouthparts called mandibles that help cut through their meal quickly.

Praying mantises will eat anything, especially other insects. Praying mantises will eat animals bigger than themselves. Big praying mantises eat frogs, lizards, birds, and even snakes!

FOOD FOR THOUGHT

Praying mantises can eat prey three times their size!

After a meal, praying mantises clean themselves with their mouth. Then they wash their head and antennae like a cat does with its front paws.

Praying mantises often eat the legs or head of an insect while it's still alive. Gross!

Mating and Cannibalism

Fall is the perfect time for praying mantises to **mate**. A male mantis finds a female and hopes she isn't hungry. The male does a dance for the female to see if she's interested. It's his way of saying he's a mate, not food!

If the female isn't hungry, they may start mating. This often takes hours and the female might get hungry. If so, the female might bite off the male's head even as they mate. Afterwards, if the male still has his head, he flies away as fast as he can because the female is surely hungry now!

This female mantis keeps a tight grip with her front legs while she takes a chunk out of her fellow mantis.

The Life Cycle

A mantis's egg case is called an ootheca (oh-uh-THEE-kuh). After winter, baby praying mantises come out of the ootheca and lower to the ground on strings of silk. They're hungry, and they often eat one another. They're a bunch of baby cannibals!

To make an ootheca, the female mantis combines eggs and foam she makes on a branch. The foam hardens into an egg case that protects the eggs during the winter.

FOOD FOR THOUGHT

There are hundreds of eggs in a praying mantis's ootheca. That's a lot of little predators!

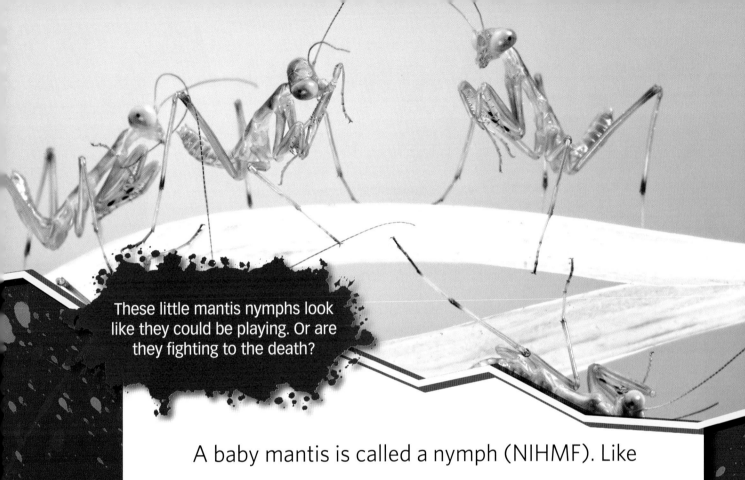

These little mantis nymphs look like they could be playing. Or are they fighting to the death?

A baby mantis is called a nymph (NIHMF). Like an adult praying mantis, a nymph has an exoskeleton. The exoskeleton doesn't grow with a praying mantis like human skin does, though. A praying mantis sheds its exoskeleton and a new, bigger exoskeleton grows in its place. This is called molting. A praying mantis molts about six times before it becomes an adult.

Praying Mantises and People

Some people keep praying mantises as pets. They enjoy watching mantises hide and hunt. After a mantis gets used to being around humans, people can even hold them. Some mantis owners let them explore and crawl on their hands. Praying mantises are wild animals, though. They might bite if they get scared or if your finger looks like prey.

Some people buy a praying mantis ootheca or nymphs to put in their garden. When they grow up into hungry mantis monsters, they'll eat all the pests in the garden. That's a natural way to keep pests away and keep mantises well fed!

Glossary

abdomen: The large, rear part of an insect's body.

defense: A feature of a living thing that helps protect it.

delicate: Easily broken.

disguise: To take on the appearance of something else in order to hide.

mate: To join together to make babies.

paralyze: To take away feeling and movement.

prey: An animal hunted by other animals for food.

protect: To keep from harm.

temperate: Not too hot or too cold.

tropical: Hot and wet.

Index

Websites

Due to the changing nature of Internet links, PowerKids Press has developed an online list of websites related to the subject of this book. This site is updated regularly. Please use this link to access the list: www.powerkidslinks.com/ancan/prma